Contact the author: m.power26@outlook.com

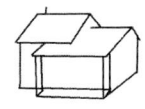

Published by the Hovel Press 2021
thehovelpress@gmail.com

Written & Illustrated by Michael Power
Designed by Roz Evans

ISBN 978-0-9956056-5-7

FOREWORD

I have treated the stories in an irreverent, but I hope not disrespectful way – sometimes with just a verse or two, sometimes with the full story. I have drawn them from the King James Version whose language is a great deal more eloquent than mine, if also rather more extended.

Our present-day concept of acceptable behaviour is quite different from that of the Old Testament. It is a bloody account which seems to accept massacres of women and children and other innocent bystanders without a qualm and no disapproval from God, who is an ever-present character. In fact he comes across as rather endearingly worried about his status. I dread to think how the Old Testament God would have reacted to same sex marriage. Fire certainly and probably a good helping of brimstone as well.

CONTENTS

1	Creation
2	God to Adam
4	The Fall & The Flood
5	The First Murder
7	Noah
10	The Camel & The Donkey
12	The Tower of Babel
14	Abraham & Isaac
18	Sodom & Gomorrah
21	Jacob & Esau
25	The Further Adventures of Jacob
29	Joseph
35	Mrs Potiphar
37	Exodus
41	The Fall of Jericho
44	Hospitality
46	The Story of Gideon
49	Samson & Delilah
54	David & Goliath
55	David & Bathsheba
58	Tamar & Ammon
59	Absalom
60	Naomi & Ruth
63	Daniel
70	Susanna & The Elders
75	Job
79	Jonah & the Whale

CREATION

God took just a week
To work on his creation.
Monday He made Day
And its dark companion, Night.
Tuesday land and sea.
Wednesday, plants and flowers
Thursday, Sun and Moon.
Friday, fishes, dolphins, whales.
Saturday was hard,
Fashioning the animals,
crowning all with Man.

That was quite a busy week,
On Sunday God said,
"I think I'll put my feet up
and have a little rest."

GOD TO ADAM

I'm giving you the right to choose
To opt for good or ill.
Essential to Humanity,
It's something called Free Will.

Now, if you are to have Free Will
You must of course have Choice
So you can choose to disregard,
Or else obey my voice.

To give you then this choice, I've made
A specialist tabu.
I'm going to tell you something that
You simply must not do.

Choice sets you above animals,
All creatures great and small.
You'd better choose what I think right.
By this you'll stand or fall.

The Tree of Knowledge stands alone
Its branches fret the sky.
Touch not the fruit of yonder Tree
For on that day, you die.

But taste that sweet yet bitter fruit
Mankind shall not be spared.
He'll move from two plus two makes four
To e is Mc squared.

Touch the flesh of that dread fruit and
You'll hear the angels crying
Your feet will tread a long hard road
A long day's dying.

Of course, they didn't die straight away, because they had to get the human race going, but Death made his entrance.

THE FALL & THE FLOOD

The serpent slid round the Knowledge Tree
And promised Eve equality.
The apple was bitten once – then twice-
And that was the end of Paradise.

That was the end of the world they knew,
Where the grass was green and the skies were blue
Now Adam must delve and Eve must spin
They have to pay for Original Sin.

Now pleasure has a partner – pain.
(Poor old Abel got whacked by Cain.)
And sin went on in the usual way
Until God's patience began to fray.

Yes, sin went on as it always will –
Flood waters covered plain, valley and hill.
Dolphins played where once elephants trod.
"You've blown it again!" boomed the voice of God.

THE FIRST MURDER

The green-eyed monster Jealousy
Devours from within.
The green-eyed monster Jealousy
Settles in your guts.
The green-eyed monster Jealousy
Drives some people nuts.

Now Cain became a farmer,
Grew food for people's tables
His vegetable marrows
Were twice the size of Abel's.

Abel was a herdsman
He had a splendid flock.
He had to keep his eye on them
All round the clock.

Both of them were pious
And sacrificed to God
Abel brought a nice fat lamb
And Cain some peas in pod.

God looked down with critic's eye
At what the two had brought
He gave a sniff and then he said
"Fat lamb is what I sought"

"Well done Abel, bad luck Cain
It's Abel who can please
A nice fat lamb is what I like
I don't care much for peas.

That really wasn't nice of God
To make the farmer frown.
It would have been much kinder
To let him gently down.

Cain took it very badly
Jealousy struck deep
He upped and slew poor Abel.
(What happened to his sheep?)

That wasn't quite the end of it,
Cain asked God for a favour.
"I'll be a general target,
I'm sorry I'm not braver."

God looked him up and down
Felt sorry for his pain,
"This mark, it will protect you,
It is the Mark of Cain."

And it did. He went off to the land of Nod where he started a new life.

NOAH

God decided that mankind was beyond hope apart from Noah, so he planned a flood which would wipe everyone out and gave Noah very precise instructions about the building of the Ark.

When Noah got given the plan
For the building of his Ark,
He scratched his head and sadly said.
"What leaves me in the dark
Is why I've got to use gopher wood.
What's the matter with larch?

Gopher wood costs twice as much
To finish every deck
I wonder if God was losing his touch
When he handed me this spec.

It's no good complaining,
The schedule has been signed
So, when it does start raining
We must not lag behind.

But still, three hundred cubits* long!
Not to mention fifty wide
And what is more I've to fit a door
Half way down the side."

Well, he and his work force finished it
The mighty craft stood tall

An endless queue came into view
All creatures great and small.

Down came the rain for forty days
(And also forty nights.)
Noah's daughters complained of their quarters
And nowhere to hang up their tights.

But then, back came the turtle dove
With an olive twig in its beak.
Just as well as the Ark was all smell
And possibly springing a leak.

The Ark grounded gently on Ararat
The animals poured from its side
Gazelles steered clear of the lions
And looked for places to hide.

Noah had had quite enough of the sea
And planted a number of vines
After which he tested and tasted
An amazing assortment of wines.

This led to an embarrassing scene
When his sons found him lying undressed
He'd collapsed on his bed as though he were dead.
He'd not even kept on his vest!
In short: He was drunk
As a skunk. **

**Even so we are told that he lived to be 950 years old, which proves that there's nothing like a drop of alcohol to keep you going.

* A cubit was 18 inches. Which makes the Ark 150 yards long and 25 yards wide.

THE CAMEL & THE DONKEY

(This not a bible story, but from the Arab world. It seems to be relevant.)

When the animals entered the ark
Noah took the very wise precaution
Of making all the male animals
Hand in their male appendage
At the cloakroom, with
The assurance that
It would be returned
In pristine condition
When they landed.
The system worked well
Considering there were a
Great many male members to store.
From gnat to elephant.
Unfortunately
There was a mix-up.
The donkey was issued
With the camel's gear.
So, when the camel turned up with his ticket
He was given the donkey's.
"I'm not having that little thing"
Sniffed the camel. And stalked off.
"You've got to!" shouted Noah
And threw it after him with
Unerring aim.

So that's why the donkey
Is so very well endowed
And why the camel wears
A supercilious expression,
And his male member
Back to front.

THE TOWER OF BABEL

In the good old days, the days when things began to pick up again after the Flood and humanity had multiplied nicely, everyone spoke the same language. However there was energy to spare once again and Noah's descendants decided on an ambitious project. They proposed to build a tower which would reach up to heaven, making them famous among other tribes. They set to work and built it so high that God became uneasy.

'They are getting a bit too close! Their pride is getting in the way of their duty to fill the Earth,' He thought, 'I'd better make things harder.'

He went straight down and scattered the impudent builders, giving each of them a different language.

"That'll teach them," said God.

What language did he say it in? Of course, I believe it was English! So now, for every speaker of each language all the other tongues were just Babel or as we say now, babble.

They obviously didn't
Have enough to do,
Those early builders.
But what a work they took on!
Making enough bricks
For a tower that was
Going to reach Heaven.
It was very imaginative of God
To put the kibosh on
The project by removing
The ability to communicate
Rather than blasting
The tower with a thunderbolt.
Furthermore, He provided a
Meal ticket for future
Language teachers
Like me.

ABRAHAM & ISAAC

Abraham was the Israelites patriarch; when he first appears he is called Abram but later is told to change his name.

Abram had a wife called Sarai who had failed to provide any children. She must have felt guilty about this, because she presented her maid, an Egyptian girl called Hagar, to her husband as a sort of consolation prize. Abram was eighty-six but nevertheless Hagar gave birth to a son called Ishmael.

Some years later, when Abram was ninety-nine, God appeared and told him that He was going to favour him and 'multiply him exceedingly'. He also told him that his name was in future to be Abraham and his wife must change her name to Sarah. He also gave a whole series of detailed instructions about circumcision. Anyone not circumcised was to be outlawed. Abraham at once gathered all the men of his household and circumcised the lot. Foreskins fell like autumn leaves.

One day a mysterious man arrived and after being fed, informed Sarah that she was going to have a son. Sarah laughed at this ridiculous suggestion. "I am old," she said, "long past the change in life." We are not told how old she was, but Abraham was at least ninety-nine.

As usual, the mysterious visitor was right and Sarah had a son called Isaac.

Sarah, who you might think would feel she was now even with Hagar, turned against her and forced Abraham to send her and Ishmael out into the desert. Hagar's water ran out so she gave herself up for dead.

However, God heard her weeping and sent an angel to tell her that not only would her son become the father of a great nation, but there was a well right beside her*. She then disappears from the story.

*The place where Hagar found the well is now the site of the Kaaba in Mecca and as we shall see, the Ishmaelites became a tribe.

God decided he needed to check up on Abraham's loyalty and spoke to him as follows:

"Take now thy son, thy only son Isaac and offer him up as a burnt offering on a mountain I shall tell thee of."

Abraham did not for a moment hesitate. They set off, father and son, with two servants and a donkey. Three days later they arrived at the place God had specified. Leaving the servants and the donkey they climbed up the mountain with Isaac carrying the wood for the burnt offering.

"We've got the wood, Father, and means of making fire," said Isaac, "but what have we got for a sacrifice?"

"God will provide a lamb," replied Abraham with sinister irony.

They reached the appointed spot and laid out the wood. Abraham tied Isaac down on the wood pyre and drew his knife.

15

An angel called out, "Abraham! Abraham!"

"Yes, that's me," said Abraham.

"God is pleased with you because you were prepared to sacrifice your only son. Look up to that thicket."

And there, caught by its horns was a fine ram, which was substituted for Isaac.

Rotten luck for the ram, at the wrong place at the wrong time.

You can't help wondering if this incident didn't colour Isaac's relationship with his father.

SACRIFICE

The sun beats down on the mountain side.
The couple climb, their movements slow
The air grows thin, few trees abide.

Chamois leap and marmots hide
Vultures soar far down below.
The sun beats down on the mountain side.

"Oh, Father shorten, please, your stride
Have we still got far to go?"
The air grows thin, few trees abide.

"Put down the wood," his father sighed
"My son, my son, I love you so."
The sun beats down on the mountain side.

A moment later he had tied
The boy he loved; had watched him grow.
The air is thin, no trees abide.

The knife is drawn; eyes open wide,
A desperate cry, "No, Father, no!"
Knife blade flashed; the old man cried,

"I have no choice, no choice, I know."
The sun beats down on the mountain side.
Then from the sky came clear and slow

A voice, "Abraham! You've not defied
God's Command. You're free to go."
The air is thin, no trees abide.

He dropped the knife and then he spied
A ram whose horns were trapped and so-
Isaac lived – the old ram died.
The sun beats down on the mountain side.

SODOM & GOMORRAH

This is the sort of story which might well appear in the tabloids today – or maybe not. Perhaps it's strong stuff, even for them.

'*Silly sod!*' is now a mild insult, but when the Marquess of Queensbury accused Oscar Wilde of being a 'somdomite' (Spelling was not his area of expertise), Wilde sued him for libel and as a result ended up in Reading Gaol convicted of gross indecency.

Abraham the patriarch was a man of tents and the open country; Lot who seems to have been an upright and virtuous citizen lived in the town of Sodom. Both Sodom and Gomorrah, cities of the plain, had the reputation of being evil places.

It was to Sodom that God sent two angels, looking like handsome, well-dressed men. It is not clear why they were there, perhaps God sent them to check up on how wicked Sodom really was.

Lot met them by the city gate. He was impressed by their appearance and invited them to stay. During the evening the men of the city came and surrounded the house:

"Send out those two dishy men we saw earlier. We really fancy them!"

"Certainly not!" said Lot, standing on his threshold, "Do not behave so wickedly."

"We'd really like to give them one up the back passage," hooted the men.

"Look," said Lot. "They are protected by the laws of hospitality, but I tell you what, I'll send out my two virgin daughters and you can do what you like with them." The men who were clearly committed homosexuals, refused this extraordinary offer and threatened to break down the door.

The angels dragged Lot back inside and used their angelic power to strike the horrible throng with blindness, which put an end to their attack.

The angels then told Lot to gather up his family and his possessions and leave the city at once. Sodom and Gomorrah were going to catch it.

"Flee!" said the angels, "and whatever you do, don't look back."

Reluctantly they fled, but Lot's wife couldn't resist having a last look at her beloved house and was instantly turned into a pillar of salt.

The story takes another extremely strange turn. Lot pleaded with God to allow him to move to another smaller city called Zoar, which He did before raining fire and brimstone on Sodom and Gomorrah.

God was not liberal when it came to homosexuality.

Lot and his two daughters were now living in a cave in Zoar; the girls discussed their future.

"Our father is old, " said the elder. "He has no wife because she has unfortunately become a pillar of salt. If we don't act our family line will die out."

"What are you suggesting?" asked the younger sister.

"We'll get Father drunk, slip into his bed and mate with him. That'll do the trick."

"All right," said her sister. "You do it tonight and I'll do it tomorrow."

And they did! They both conceived, both bore sons, one called Moab and the other Ben-ammi.

Moab's father was also his grandpa,
whose wife was a pillar of salt.
Did Lot know what had happened?
Did he know of this sexual assault?
What I find surprising
What makes this tale seem tall;
If he was so extremely drunk
How he managed it at all.

JACOB & ESAU

Here is another story of deceit and trickery. God does not seem to have been bothered by the behaviour of one of the fathers of the Israelites.

In her old age, Isaac's wife, Rebekah gave birth to twins. The firstborn was covered in hair, the second to emerge was smooth and hairless. The first born was Esau and the second, Jacob.

As they grew up Esau became old Isaac's favourite while Rebekah loved Jacob.

Esau was a keen hunter, Jacob more of a stay-at-home. One day Esau came back from hunting, dog-tired and hungry.

"Give me some of that red pottage, Jacob. I'm starving."

"All right," said Jacob, "but you must promise to hand over your birthright."

"I'm dying of hunger," said Esau. "What use is my birthright if I die? Give me some of that pottage and you can have it."

"Swear!" said Jacob.

"I swear."

I'm not clear what the birthright was. Presumably it meant the firstborn's right of inheritance. Was Esau wrong to hand over his birthright so casually? He couldn't have been literally dying of hunger after a day's hunting. He seems to have been a rather impulsive character.

So now Jacob owned the birthright which should have gone to the eldest son.

Isaac was getting very old and very blind, and feeling he hadn't much time left he asked Esau to hunt a deer and make him a savoury dish of venison.

"I love this dish and I will give you my exclusive blessing before I die."

Rebekah overheard and called Jacob.

"Go out," she said, "fetch two kids from the goat herd and I'll make them into a savoury stew which you can take to your father, pretending to be Esau. Then you'll get the blessing."

"But, mother," objected Jacob, "Esau is a hairy man and I am a smooth man. He may not be able to see me, but he can certainly feel that I'm not hairy. He'll call me a deceiver and curse me."

"Just do as I say," said his devoted mother, "I'll use the goatskins to cover your hands and neck, and you must put on Esau's clothes so you smell right."

She cooked a delicious dish of young kid and told Jacob to carry it into his father.

"Who has brought me this delicious food?"

"Me, father - Esau," said Jacob. "Now eat your venison stew and then you can give me your exclusive blessing."

"You caught the deer very quickly," said Isaac suspiciously.

"Er... God guided me," said Jacob, thinking quickly.

"Come nearer, my son, so I can feel whether you are really Esau. Your voice is very like Jacob's."

Jacob approached him and Isaac felt the goat skin "Your hands are the hands of Esau and your clothes smell of Esau. Here is my blessing:"

> *See the smell of my son*
> *Is the smell of the field which the Lord hath blessed.*
> *Therefore, God give thee of the dew of heaven*
> *And the fatness of the earth*
> *And plenty of corn and wine:*
> *Let the people serve thee*
> *And nations bow down to thee.*

Jacob cleared away the plate and went off delighted with the success of the ruse.

A little later Esau arrived with a venison stew:

"Father, come and eat the venison dish you asked for and then you can give me your blessing."

"What!" cried old Isaac, "Who are you?"

"I'm Esau, your eldest son."

"Who was that who brought me a venison stew just now? I gave him my exclusive blessing."

"Oh my God!" shouted Esau. "That's twice! He got me to hand over my birthright and now he's cheated me of my blessing."

"I know" said Isaac sadly. "I have made him your senior; I have made all your brothers his servants and left him cornfields and vineyards. What is there left to give you?"

"Have you no blessing for me, then, my father?" asked Esau, now weeping openly.

Isaac did the best he could – but of course it was not nearly so powerful a blessing. Esau so hated his brother that he swore to kill him.

Rebekah got wind of this and sent Jacob to stay with her brother Laban...

"Just till it all blows over."

Surprisingly, Isaac doesn't seem to blame Jacob, and sends him off with his blessing again and tells him to take a wife from among Laban's daughters, his cousins.

Jacob set off to seek his fortune.

MOTHER LOVE

Rebekah dearly loved her son
The second of the twins.
There's nothing she would not have done
To ensure that that son won.
Rebekah dearly loved her son.
Cheating, lying- all were one
To make sure Jacob wins.
For as long as time's sands run,
Rebekah dearly loves her son.

THE FURTHER ADVENTURES OF JACOB

Jacob set off to his uncle's place and on the way had a curious dream. He dreamt that there was a ladder which reached from the earth to heaven. Angels were climbing up and down it and above the ladder stood God.

"Jacob! I give you this land you are sleeping on and land to the North, South, East and West. I shall be on your side, Jacob, I shall not leave you till I have done all I have promised!"

Jacob thought this looked encouraging and set up a pillar as a memorial to his dream of the ladder (Jacob's Ladder).

He arrived at Uncle Laban's house and was made welcome – it seems to have been agreed that he would work for his living, looking after the sheep and cattle.

Now Laban had two daughters, Leah the elder who was 'tender-eyed' and Rachel who was more beautiful. Jacob agreed with Laban that he would work for seven years without pay after which he would be given Rachel as his wife.

Jacob worked hard for seven years and the wedding was arranged.

But Laban obviously had some of his sister's cunning because he dressed tender-eyed Leah in a heavy veil and presented her as the bride. So, Jacob found himself married to her. When he complained, Laban told him that it was customary for the elder daughter to be married first and that was that.

So now it was Jacob who was on the wrong end of a trick.

However, he was a stayer. Laban offered him Rachel in return for another seven years' work and Jacob agreed.

After the time was up, Jacob had two wives, one he loved and one he hated. But the irony was that the one he hated kept having sons while Rachel, whom he loved, was barren.

Jacob also had sons by various handmaidens, but it was not until very late in life that Rachel ate some mandrake root, promptly conceived and gave birth to a son who was named Joseph.

(Famous biblical characters often seem to be born to elderly mothers. Is this significant?)

Time went by and Jacob decided he could safely go home to his mother.

"We've done well since you've been here," said Laban. "What wages would you like?"

"I would like to take all the speckled and spotted sheep, if that's not asking too much" replied Jacob.

"Very reasonable," said Laban.

Jacob had another cunning plan, though. He took a large number of green hazel sticks and peeled rings of bark off them, so that they were striped with white.

He set them up in view of the pregnant ewes which, of course, resulted in all their lambs being speckled or spotted.

His ruse was so successful that he was able to take most of Laban's flock. Laban and his sons resented this but Jacob claimed they were his due.

So Jacob gathered everything together including Leah and Rachel who purloined several of her father's God images and they stole away in the night. Laban was incensed by this behaviour and chased after them. When he caught up he said to Jacob, more in sorrow than in anger:

"Why did you sneak off in the night? We could have had a feast and celebration to mark your departure and singing and music and I could have kissed my daughters good-bye. Furthermore, someone has stolen my God images."

Jacob replied, "I was afraid you wouldn't allow your daughters to leave and that you would take them from me. As for your images… if we find the thief, we will put him to death!"

Laban went round the camp searching and got to Leah's tent. Nothing there.

He then went to Rachel's tent. Rachel had hidden the images in the camel saddle-bags she was sitting on. Laban asked her stand up so that he could check them, but she claimed she couldn't because she was having her period. Embarrassed at hearing this intimate detail Laban backed off and left without finding his images.

This failure put Laban onto the back foot. Jacob seized the advantage and embarked on a long rant about what a hard time he had had with Laban, how he had worked his fingers to the bone in every kind of weather for pitiful wages which were constantly being revised.

This seems to have worked, for Laban very generously offered to make peace, and they parted on amicable terms.

Jacob with his many sheep, cattle and servants then set off for home.

MORE TRICKERY

Jacob was a trickster.
God didn't seem to mind.
Whatever Jacob did
God was right behind.

Seven years he laboured
Without any wage.
Married the wrong sister
Which put him in a rage.

But he got his own back
With ingenious tricks.
Plundered Laban's flocks of sheep
With forests of peeled sticks.

JOSEPH

The Story of Joseph and his brothers is well-known from the work of Rice and Lloyd-Webber, but I'm going to tell it just the same.

Joseph was the child of Jacob and Rachel's old age, and Jacob loved him dearly. As a mark of this preference, he made Joseph a 'coat of many colours'. This clear favouritism rankled with the numerous brothers born to Leah. Joseph who, as we shall see later, was not a tactful man, insisted on recounting his latest dream to his brothers. Of course, other people's dreams are usually boring but this one was particularly annoying.

"I dreamt," said Joseph, "that we were all harvesting and binding sheaves of corn in the field. My sheaf stood upright, while all your sheaves gathered round and bowed to it."

This obviously displeased the brothers but Joseph hadn't finished; he dreamt that the sun, moon and eleven stars all bowed down to him. He insisted on telling his father and brothers about this and his father rebuked him:

"Are you saying that you are going to have dominion over me and your mother and all your brothers? I rather think not."

A little later Joseph was sent after his brothers who were grazing their sheep some days' journey way away. The brothers saw him coming from far off.

"Now's our chance! We'll kill him, throw him in a pit and tell Father that a wild beast ate him."

But Reuben, the eldest, was against this.

"No, don't kill him, just throw him in a pit, we don't want blood on our hands."

Joseph arrived, was stripped of his many-coloured coat and deposited in a deep pit. At this point a caravan of Ishmaelites on their way to Egypt came by.

"How about selling Joseph to these men?" suggested Judah. "That way we won't be shedding any blood and we'll make a few shekels."

"Good thinking!" said the brothers, and that is what they did. What's more, they got twenty pieces of silver.

The brothers dipped the many-coloured coat in goat's blood and took it back to Jacob, telling him that Joseph had been eaten by wild animals. Jacob believed them and gave way to bitter grief.

In Egypt an important official called Potiphar bought Joseph as a slave, and employed him in his house. He made himself so useful that he was soon running the household – a sort of indispensable major-domo.

But it was too good to last – Potiphar's wife took a fancy to him. He refused her proposition indignantly. She responded by crying out, "Rape!"

Joseph was dragged off to prison. Surprisingly he was not executed and was well treated in prison becoming a sort of 'trusty'.

Two inmates, the Pharoah's butler and baker, who had displeased their master by serving up stale croissants, started dreaming. Who better to interpret these dreams than Joseph?

He interpreted the butler's rather obscure dream to mean that the butler was going to be released in three days.

The baker's dream was that he was carrying three baskets of pastries for the Pharoah on his head when a flock of birds came and ate them.

"That's easy," said Joseph, "Three baskets – three days. In three days the Pharoah is going to remove your head."

Sure enough, three days later that's what happened. The butler got his job back and the baker was executed.

Then Pharoah started dreaming. First of all, that seven fat cattle came up out of the river, pursued by seven lean cattle which devoured the fat ones.

The next night Pharoah dreamt along the same lines, only this time it was seven mangy ears of corn which consumed the seven good ears.

Pharoah was sure that these dreams must have some important meaning but his magicians and soothsayers were baffled. However, the butler remembered Joseph's success from two years before and Pharoah had him brought up from the prison.

"That's the same dream," explained Joseph. "The seven cows and the seven ears of corn are seven years. The fat cattle and fat ears represent plentiful harvests which will be followed by seven years of famine."

For the first seven years surplus corn was planted and stored in warehouses, so that when the famine years followed there was corn in Egypt. Jospeh was rewarded by being made governor, second only to the Pharoah himself.

Back in Canaan, famine had struck, so Jacob sent the ten elder brothers to Egypt to buy food.

Joseph was now governor of Egypt and when the brothers arrived he recognised them but made sure they didn't know him. They treated him with great respect but Joseph spoke roughly.

"Where are you lot from?"

"From Canaan, your Honour. We've come to buy food."

"I fancy you're a bunch of spies, come to see how poor we are."

"No, Your Honour, truly, we have just come to buy food. We were twelve brothers, there's a young one called Benjamin, staying with our father and one has disappeared."

Joseph said, "This is what you'll do to prove you're telling the truth. Send for your youngest brother. Leave one of you here as a hostage, take what corn you need, and bring your young brother back here."

Simeon was bound over as a hostage and the remaining brothers set off home. To their surprise and alarm, they found the money they had paid stuffed in the corn sacks. What was going on?

When they got home Jacob refused to let them take Benjamin back to Egypt. Simeon the hostage had certainly died, so what was the point?

But the famine continued, the corn ran out and Jacob was persuaded to let them take Benjamin with them back to Egypt. This time Joseph entertained them royally, feasting them in his own house and again sent them off with the money they had brought. But that would have been far too simple. He told a servant to hide a valuable silver cup in Benjamin's sack and after the brothers had left he sent men after them, to accuse them of stealing his cup.

The brothers hotly protested their innocence: "If you find the cup in one of our sacks its owner shall die." The cup was duly found. Joseph announced that the thief, Benjamin, should be his servant, the others could go home.

Judah then made an impassioned plea, explaining that the boy was the only son remaining to Rachel. The loss of his favourite child would certainly kill the old man and he, Judah, would gladly take the boy's place.

Joseph could hold out no longer. He dismissed all the Egyptians present and revealed himself to the brothers.

There was then a great reconciliation scene. Joseph said God must have planned the whole thing. He sent for his father and all his father's flocks and herds and settled them in the Egyptian district of Goshen. Jacob was by no means done for, he lived another seventeen years and died at the age of a hundred and forty-seven. He was also known as Israel and the tribe that settled and multiplied and prospered in Egypt are, from now on, referred to as the Children of Israel or Israelites rather than Hebrews.

So, a happy ending.

Except that four hundred years later they made their great escape as recounted in Exodus.

JOSEPH AND HIS BAD TASTE COAT

I don't warm to Joseph, I feel, in fact
He could have kept a lid on his dreams.
Wherever he goes he always seems
To be totally lacking in tact.

His dreams are simply all too clear.
His brothers' sheaves all bowing low!
Sun, moon and stars to him also!
His dreams are going to cost him dear.

And then there was his show-off coat
He probably wore it to bed.
Not surprising his brothers said,
"Let's slit his effing throat."

In the end they didn't commit that crime
They sold him at quite a good price.
And then, another roll of the dice
And the remorseless passage of time

Finds him giving old Potiphar's wife
The rougher edge of his tongue.
Because he was pretty, because he was young
He got away with his life.

I suppose his brothers deserved a fright
For selling him off as they did.
But all that tricking the young Benjamin
Doesn't really seem right.

MRS POTIPHAR

Potiphar was a mandarin,
Adviser to the Pharoah.
Orders out and orders in,
So Pharoah had no care-o.

But Potiphar, he had a wife.
Supple, slim and fair-o.
She was trouble, she was strife
All danger she would dare-o.

If you should chance to catch her eye
You'd better beware-o.
If you do not want to die,
Leg it like a hare-o

Now Joseph working as a slave
Was a handsome fellow.
Mrs P. gave him a wave.
His legs gave way like jello.

"Come here, come here, Joseph my dear
I'd like to get to know you."
Come to my boudoir, never fear
There's something I must show you,"

"Oh madam I well know my place
I have my maser's trust-o.
I am surprised you have the face
To advertise your lust-o."

Oh foolish Joseph, where's your tact?

Why not plead a cold-o?
At once the lady's good mood cracked
That he should be so bold-o.

She gave a scream, she gave a shriek
And then her clothes did tear-o.
"It's rape!" she yelled, "I cannot speak!
I'd nothing left to wear-o"

What good for Joseph to protest?
Let him weep and wail-o
Her word of course was deemed the best,
They hauled him off to jail-o.

Still, he didn't lose his head
His life the judge did spare-o.
In prison dreams he rightly read
Endeared him to the Pharoah.

EXODUS

The story of the Israelites escape from Egypt is a dramatic one.

This is the background:

The Pharoah who employed Joseph was long gone and another Pharoah ruled. The Israelites meanwhile had enormously multiplied, to a point which worried the Egyptian authorities- lest they should be outnumbered in their own country. The new policy was to be one of extreme harshness; the Israelites were to do all the heavy labour – and even that was made more arduous wherever possible. They had to make bricks but were deliberately given no binding straw – Pharoah ordered the city midwives to kill all the male Israelite babies. An order which the midwives failed to carry out. They claimed that the Israeli women were more 'lively' than Egyptian women and gave birth before the midwives could get to them.

At this point Moses enters the scene as a baby. Another Pharoahic order was that male Israelite babies should be thrown into the Nile. Moses' mother couldn't bring herself to do this, so put him in a floating cradle which lodged among the bulrushes on the riverbank. Here, by an amazing stroke of luck, he was found by Pharoah's daughter. She was a kindly girl and paid for a wet-nurse to look after the baby.

Another Pharoah continued to oppress the Hebrews (Israelites) and God decided that enough was enough.

He spoke to Moses, now grown up, from the interior of a burning bush and he told him that he was going to present the Israelites with a land 'flowing with milk and honey'- The Promised Land.

"Now," said God, "Go to Pharoah and tell him you propose to take the Israelites out of Egypt."

"Who… me?" Moses was aghast.

"Of course he will refuse," said God, "But I shall smite the Egyptians with my wonders, and after that he will let you go."

Moses put the request to Pharoah who refused as expected and ordered even harsher labour conditions for the Hebrews. Moses returned to have a sharp word with God.

"Why did you send me to Pharoah? It just made things worse."

"Don't worry," said God. "I am going to get you out of here and into the Promised Land. Then you will know that I am your true God and when I've finished with the Egyptians, they will know too!"

He was as good as his word. He polluted the water of the Nile so that the Egyptians had nothing to drink but somehow managed to get water to the Israelites.

He then told Moses to try again. "Let my people go!" If you don't, I'll send a plague of frogs who will die and stink. I'll turn the dust of the desert into lice. I'll send swarms of flies." Which He did. He even made sure all the Egyptian cattle died while sparing the Hebrews' cows.

Pharoah remained extremely stubborn in the face of all these disasters and continued to refuse to let the Hebrews go.

Oddly, the Bible story claims that God 'hardened Pharoah's heart' so that he refused the Israelites leave to depart. What was the point of that?

Then the Hebrews were given instructions for the great escape. They were to get ready to leave and mark their doors with lamb's blood then stay indoors. God proceeded to kill the firstborn in every house, sparing only the houses which had blood marking their doors.

"Now you can go," said God. "But before you go borrow as much cash and jewellery from the Egyptians as you can." Amazingly the Egyptians came up with a load of valuables which was extremely generous in the circumstances, although they thought it was just a loan.

The Israelites then set of at night, taking with them their flocks and herds (and stuff they had 'borrowed' from the Egyptians) after a stay in Egypt, according to Exodus, of four hundred and thirty years.

Pharoah, as soon as he heard of the departure sent his army in pursuit. The Israelites were trapped on the shores of the Red Sea, but God quickly parted the waters so that they could cross. When they were safely on the other side, He let the water back which drowned the whole pursuing Egyptian army – every single man.

The Israelites set out on what was to be a forty-year journey to The Promised Land.

EXODUS

Yes, it must have been
A bit like South African apartheid,
So that if you were an Israelite
You were expected to do all the heavy work
Like making bricks from mud
Without straw.
And for four hundred years
They sweated tears and blood.
Then God had a word with Moses,
And made him understand
That He now proposes
To give them the Promised Land.
Pharoah refused, at any price,
To let the Hebrews go.
God sent plagues of frogs and lice
And a final cruel blow -
Destroyed every eldest son
In each Egyptian home.
Now the Israelites can run,
for forty years they'll roam
In wilderness and desert sand
Before they reach
Their Promised Land.

THE FALL OF JERICHO

After the death of Moses, who had led the Israelites during their forty years of wandering in the wilderness, leadership went to Joshua. Under him the Israelites were going to be allowed to occupy the Promised Land but first they had to deal with Jericho, a populous city which stood in their way.

Joshua began by sending out a couple of spies to report back on the defences. They seem to have been rather unprofessional because they visited a sex-worker called Rahab whose house was on the city wall and they were spotted.

Two security men duly arrived to arrest them but Rahab had got wind of this. She told the spies that she had heard great things about the Israelites and their extremely powerful god. She was particularly impressed by the story of the parting of the Red Sea to allow the great escape from Egypt. So she offered to hide them hoping that, in return, they would deal kindly with her and her family if the Israelites took Jericho.

"We have reason to believe according to our very reliable sources that you are concealing two suspicious persons. Kindly lead us to them!"

Rahab replied, "No sir, there were two men here, but they have gone. If you are quick you can probably overtake them."

"That's as may be but if you don't mind, madam, we'll take a look around!"

But Rahab had hidden the men well under some bales of flax and after the security men left, she let them down off the wall on a rope. Before they went, they told her to tie a scarlet ribbon in the window so that her house would be spared in the coming attack.

Now Joshua set his plan in motion but not before God had given him a helping hand by holding up the water of the Jordan to let the tribe pass.

Child's play compared with the parting the Red Sea.

These were God's instructions which were relayed by Joshua:

The warriors were to march round the city once a day for six days.
With them will go seven priests bearing trumpets.

On the seventh day they were to march round the city seven times and then the priests were to blow their trumpets, everyone will give a great shout upon which, the walls will fall down flat allowing the warriors easy entrance.

It worked like charm and went exactly according to plan. Down fell the walls, the warriors rushed the city and slew everyone, men, women and children, oxen, asses, chickens – nothing was spared except for Rahab and her family who had put a scarlet ribbon in their window.

I suppose this gave Gideon his idea for wiping out the Midianites. The trumpets seem to be the key, amazing instruments whose e-sharp could set your teeth on edge from ten miles away. What would Louis Armstrong and Miles Davies and Dizzy Gillespie have given for trumpets like these?

THE FALL OF JERICHO

Poor old Jericho
Where thousands died.
All because God
Was on the other side.

Joshua was adamant
No softie bleeding heart.
"Go on," he said "When all are dead
Then we can depart."

Whoever Israel's army smote
Jolly well stayed smitten.
Watch out you other cities -
Be twice shy if once bitten.

HOSPITALITY

The Israelites were once again at war with their neighbours. The outcome always depended on how well or badly they had been behaving. God either delivered them into the hands of their enemies or vice versa.

The Canaanites under their general Sisera who had a force of nine hundred iron chariots had the upper hand for years until God backed the Israelites under Barak who completely wiped out Sisera's army and the nine hundred chariots.

Sisera fled the field and reached the tent of Heber the Kenite and his wife Jael.

Presumably Sisera didn't know where the Kenite sympathies lay or assumed he would not be recognised.

Jael comes to the door of the tent

"Good day, sir – Can I help you?"

Sisera introduces himself, "Good day madam- I am a weary traveller. Could I trouble you for a cup of water?"

Jael recognises him, "Come in sir, come in! You are most welcome. Lie down here and I will bring you something to drink." She brings him a cup of milk and scones with butter.

Sisera said, "You're an angel. Would you mind standing at the entrance and if anyone comes asking, tell them there's no one here."

"Of course I will. Now you get some sleep." Sisera was very grateful and fell asleep at once.

Jael went out of the tent, picked up a tent peg and a heavy mallet and went back into the tent. She took the peg and placed the tip carefully against the sleeping man's temple and then gave it a terrific whack, so that it went clean though his head and pinned him to the ground.

The captain of the men pursuing Sisera arrived, took in the scene, then asked, "Did you do that?"

"I did... What is it? Why are you looking at me like that?"

The prophetess Deborah was impressed and wrote this poem, as it appears in the King James Version of the Bible.

> The wife of Heber the Kenite,
> Blessed shall she be above women in the tent.
> He asked for water and she gave him milk
> She brought forth butter in a lordly dish.
> She put her hand to the nail,
> And her hand to the workman's hammer:
> And with the hammer she smote Sisera, she smote off his head
> When she had pierced and stricken through his temples,
> At her feet he bowed, he fell, he lay down
> Where he bowed, there he fell down dead.

THE STORY OF GIDEON

The Israelites went to war again – this time with the Midianites who descended upon them like swarm of locusts. Of course, the Israelites had been misbehaving again and to begin with, God let them suffer. Then after seven years he relented and chose Gideon to fight for them against the Midianites.

Gideon seems to have been an extremely cautious man, and he rather cheekily bargained with God:

"I'm sorry to bother you, Lord, but could you give me a sign that you really will back me up?"

"What sort of sign my son?" God was curious.

"I'll put out a fleece tonight, and if in the morning the fleece is wet with dew, but the earth round it is dry, I'll know you really mean it."

Gideon placed the fleece and the next morning, sure enough, the ground was dry and the fleece was soaking wet.

Now most people would have let it go at that, but Gideon was ultra-careful and risked asking God to reverse the process by leaving a dry fleece on dew-wet ground. Unusually good-natured, God did not smite Gideon but did what he asked. Gideon was now convinced that the Lord was with him.

He addressed the tribe and said that anyone who wasn't up for a fight should go back to their tents. Twenty-two thousand departed. One thousand remained.

God stepped in again, telling Gideon how to run a selection scheme.

Take the men to the river and bid them drink. Some will lap the water from their cupped hands, and some will lie on their stomachs and drink straight from the stream… you must take the ones that lap as your commando.

Three hundred men passed the test, and this little force gazed down at the Midianites in the valley, as numerous as a swarm of locusts. Gideon now gave his orders.

Every man must arm himself and carry in his left hand a trumpet and in his right an earthenware pot with a lighted lamp inside it.

On my command you will blow the trumpet and break the pot so that the lamp shines out. Then shout out:

'The sword of the Lord and of Gideon!'

This was a psychological master stroke. The noise, the sudden light and the shouting so confused the Midianites in the darkness that they started fighting each other. The result was the massacre of the Midianites.

Gideon became king and looted one thousand seven hundred shekels of gold from the Midianites. This made him so extremely rich that he could afford many wives and several concubines with whom he fathered seventy sons.

However, believe it or not, as soon as he died the Israelites went a-whoring after Baal again. They never seemed to learn.

GIDEON'S ATTACK

From the blackness of the night
A mighty roar
And blinding light.
No wonder
The Midianites took fright.
They didn't know
Friend from foe
Or who to fight.

All was shouting and confusion-
There would be just one conclusion.
Without the chance of flight
The Midianites, that mighty horde,
One and all, put to the sword.
Not a single soul survives.
Men, women, children,
All lost their lives.

SAMSON & DELILAH

Samson's mother was thought to be unable to have children, but late in life she gave birth to a boy. An angel gave her the following instructions.

    a) She must not touch alcohol during her pregnancy.
    b) No scissors or razor to be allowed near his hair, as he is a Nazarite.

"Furthermore," said the angel, "he will deliver the Israelites from the Philistines." (Who were ruling over the Israelites at the time.)

The boy grew up and fell for a Philistine woman. He asked his father to arrange for him to marry her, which his father reluctantly did.

While his father was negotiating, Samson killed a lion with his bare hands; this was so easy he never bothered to mention it.

Later he was on his way to his wedding when he passed a dead lion in whose carcase a swarm of bees had nested. Samson and his parents feasted on honey and this gave Samson his idea for his famous riddle. He invited thirty young men to the wedding and before the ceremony he challenged them to answer it.

'Out of the eater came forth meat.
Out of the strong came forth sweetness.'

"You have three days," he told them, "to answer my riddle. If you fail you must give me thirty sheets and thirty suits of clothes. If you solve it I will do the same for you."

The young men were baffled so they went to the new wife and threatened her, forcing her to wheedle the answer out of Samson.

The wife started to put pressure on Samson. She wept and cried for a whole week while the marriage celebrations were going on until poor Samson told her the answer, which she passed on to the young men.

They went to Samson and said:

> "What is sweeter than honey?
> And what is stronger than a lion?"

Samson raised his eyebrows in disbelief, replying:

> "If you had not ploughed with my heifer
> You had not found out my riddle."

He paid up, as he promised, by going to the nearest Philistine town, slaying thirty men, and taking their possessions.

Time went by. Samson, who seems to have travelled a lot, came home to find his father-in-law had given his wife to another man. Samson complained, but his father-in-law said "I thought you hated her. Take her younger sister instead, she's prettier anyhow."

Samson didn't accept this and had another go at the Philistines by catching two foxes, tying their tails together, fixing a burning brand between them and letting them loose in the Philistine cornfields.

"Now we're quits," said Samson.

But the story takes an odd turn; the men of Judah, currying favour with the ruling Philistines, went to Samson and asked if they could bind him. "We will not harm you. But we've got to hand you over to the Philistines who are ruling us."

Samson agreed and allowed them to bind him with new cords and take him to the Philistines.

The Philistines were delighted to have laid their hands on Samson, but they hadn't reckoned on his amazing strength. He snapped the ropes like cotton thread, picked up the jawbone of an ass and proceeded to slaughter a thousand men. He was a bit tired and thirsty after this but God gave him a drink and he felt much better.

Unfortunately Samson was a slow learner and he fell in love with a beauty called Delilah.

The Philistines offered her eleven hundred pieces of silver if she could discover the secret of his great strength. That was good money, and Delilah determined to earn it.

"Tell me I pray thee, Samson, the secret of thy great strength."

"If thou should bind me with seven green withies, I would become weak." Samson said.

Delilah tied him up with green withies, and cried, "The Philistines are upon thee Samson!"

Samson shrugged his shoulders and the withies snapped like rotten twigs.

"You're just making fun of me, Samson, tell me the truth!"

"All right. If you were to tie me up with brand new rope that has never been used before, then I will be as weak as any other man."

The same procedure as before. Delilah tied him up and shouted:

"The Philistines are upon thee Samson!"

Samson snapped the rope as easily as if it had been a thread of flax and the Philistines stayed put.

"I knew it! You don't love me at all. If you loved me you wouldn't lie to me."

And she nagged him, day and night till he could stand it no longer and told her that the secret of his strength lay in his hair.

He seems to have quite forgotten his earlier experience with the first wife and his riddle.   I suppose he thought Delilah was joking when she shouted that the Philistines were upon him.

Delilah waited until he had fallen asleep, his trusting head in her lap, and cut away his hair.

Once again she shouted:

"The Philistines be upon thee Samson!"

This time he was no stronger than any ordinary man and the Philistines captured him easily. They put out his eyes, dragged him down to Gaza and set him to work grinding corn.

Years passed and Samson's hair grew back.

A great Philistine festival was held and blind Samson was brought from his mill as a trophy, as something to be mocked. The great hall with its galleries was crowded with holiday makers, some beneath, some above the two huge pillars which held the building up.

Samson, the object of their mockery, was tied between the pillars. The Philistines laughed but Samson gripped the pillars, one in either arm and with a grunt he strained to close is arms. A creak, a crack, the pillars gave way and down came the galleries upon the floor beneath. The death toll was terrible. In his dying Samson slew more than in his life.

Nazarite born, Nazarite bred
Strong in the arm, but weak in the head.

Delilah's song
Lay thy weary head, my love
Gently on my knee,
Let sweet sleep steal softly
As I sing to thee.

A song that's from my childhood
An ancient nursery air.
Sleep my love, sleep deeply --
While I cut your hair.

DAVID & GOLIATH

David was a shepherd boy who had been sent up to the front with food for his brothers in the Israelite army. When he heard the challenge to single combat issued by Goliath, he at once volunteered. Obviously this was regarded as ridiculous, but David told King Sail about his conquests of various wild beasts, which proved that God was on his side. Reluctantly Sail gave his permission.

There stands huge Goliath,
armoured like a tank.
Single combat
On the river bank.
One man will stay standing.
One will fall.
The tribe whose champion triumphs
Takes it all.
Here stoops the shepherd boy
All on his own,
Picking from the flashing stream
A smooth river stone.
"Am I dog?" Hear Goliath roar.
"That a boy can face me
With stones and nothing more? "
Then comes a hum as swings the sling.
Hear the speeding missile sing
like a wasp with lethal sting.
The giant lifts his weighty sword
Now it's come to blows-
But deadly pebble cracks his skull.
Crash! Bang! down he goes.
From the watching Philistines
Rises up a groan -
Their champion has been destroyed
By shepherd lad, alone.

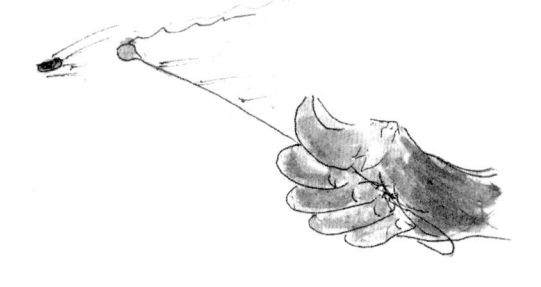

DAVID & BATHSHEBA

Of the SEVEN DEADLY SINS
Third comes LUST
Which may well be the deadliest
Turning 'want' to 'must'.

King David stood on his palace roof
And gazed across his town.
In the middle distance
Something held his gaze
A lovely woman bathing
In early morning haze,
What was it held him? What did he see?
Curve of hip, swell of breast or a lock of hair?
That was the beginning of
A deadly affair.

The woman was married.
Bathsheba her name.
King David had her sent for,
So naturally she came.
David was all-powerful
He said, "I must insist!"
Bathsheba, his subject.
How could she resist?

And David did a dreadful thing
An act unworthy of a king
Displayed his fatal flaw.
King David told his general
"Send Uriah to the front.
Where the fighting's fiercest
Where he'll bear the brunt
Of enemy charges, enemy's attack -
See to it General, I don't want him back."

It worked of course; Uriah died
Bathsheba now King David's bride.
In due course they had a son
And they named him Solomon.

But God was watching. Deeply shocked,
Planned retribution. "God's not mocked."

Sent Prophet Nathan, man to man:
"Listen David, to this tale…
A poor man had a much-loved lamb,
His only one, it shared his home
His food, his bed and without fail
He nurtured it most tenderly.

A rich man who had flocks galore
Cattle, goats and much, much more.
Took the lamb without request
And cooked that lamb to feed a guest".

Cried David, "Villain! Scoundrel! Thief!
I cannot bear that poor man's grief.
I will seek him, low and high
That evil man must surely die."

Then Nathan spoke, "You are that man.
Uriah died. That was your plan.
Now God is going to make you pay
God will make you rue that day
Marked in history's recorder
The day you gave the murder order."

TAMAR & AMMON

This is a rather unpleasant story of unbridled lust and rape.

Ammon, like Absalom, was one of King David's sons, who fell desperately in love with Tamar who is referred to as Absalom's sister – presumably she was Ammon's sister too or perhaps his half-sister.

He was advised by his crafty friend Johadab to pretend to be sick, ask Tamar to bring him some food in his bedroom and then to see what happens.

RAPE

Ammon lay, crafty sick
Nursing his obsession.
Unsuspecting Tamar
Brought him food,
Sick room food,
Quite glad of the digression.

Ammon came straight to the point
There was no hesitation.
"Come to bed!" is what he said.
"Let's use this situation."
She answered boldly, "In your dreams!"
He grabbed her hair, dragged her to bed.
No-one heard her screams.

When he'd done, had his fun
Ammon felt revulsion.
He kicked her out, "Arise. Begone!
Don't say I used compulsion."

When Absalom was told the tale
He bade her keep to silence.
Family honour must prevail,
No talk of Ammon's violence.

So, Ammon got away scot-free.
For honour, name and such-
'Oh, ancient days,' we say. But we
Haven't changed that much.

ABSALOM

Absalom was handsome with a perfect physique
His hair was thick and shining, wonderfully sleek.
David loved him dearly, more than all his sons
Favoured him always or so the story runs,
But David has a debt to pay: the death of Uriah
Now it has fallen due. No price could be higher.

Treacherous rebellion by the favourite son
This is David's punishment -thus the tale was spun,
Ungrateful Absalom takes up arms
 Gathers men of Israel from cities and from farms.
Battle's joined. Bloody work, - scenes from Hell
David's men victorious, but bitter news to tell:
Absalom was riding fast through Ephraim wood
Before him unnoticed an oak tree stood.
 In a branch's fork his handsome head was caught,
His mule galloped on; the rider brought up short
Left hanging helpless, dangling in the air.
Little use to him now his fine head of hair!
David's general Joab gave him the *coup de grace*
Then was David told: "Thus it came to pass"
That was the end of it. The story was done
But out rang the stricken cry:
"O Absalom my son!
Would that I had died for thee,
O Absalom my son!" *

Last line from the Book of Samuel

NAOMI & RUTH

An antidote to mother-in-law jokes .

Once upon a time there was a woman from Judah who married a Moabite and went with him to live in Moab *(modern-day Jordan)*.

Her name was Naomi, she had two sons who married Moabite girls: Orpah and Ruth. Naomi's husband died and then, not long after, both her sons also died. She was left to live with her two daughters-in-law.

She told them to leave her and go back to their families as she was going to return to Judah. Orpah eventually agreed, but Ruth was determined to stay with her mother-in-law.

"Whither thou goest, I will go, whither thou lodgest, I will lodge. Thy people shall be my people...."

They returned together to Judah with no money, and very few possessions. Luckily It was the time of the barley harvest and Naomi got permission for Ruth to glean odd ears of barley dropped by the harvesters.

Now it so happened that the field in which she was gleaning belonged to a rich farmer called Boaz, a relative of Naomi's. Boaz noticed Ruth, a stranger, and asked about her. He was told that she was a Moabitess and had come with her mother-in law to live in Judah.

Ruth was an attractive young woman, and Boaz invited her to work with his maidens. "I have forbidden my young men to hassle you," he told her.

"Why," asked Ruth, "are you showing me such favour?"

"Because you have been so loyal to Naomi." He told his harvesters to drop plenty of ears of barley, as though by mistake.

When Ruth got home with an armful of corn, she told Naomi about the kindness of Boaz.

"Boaz! He's a relation of mine"

Now the story takes an odd turn.

"Listen," said Naomi, "Tonight, put on your best dress and make-up, go down to Boaz's house, but don't make yourself known. Find out where Boaz is sleeping and when he has gone to bed slip in and lie down at his feet."

Ruth did as she was told. She sneaked in, uncovered his feet and lay down.

Boaz woke in the night, feeling there was something strange going on. To his astonishment he saw there was a woman lying at his feet.

"What! What! Who on earth are you?"

"It's all right," said Ruth. "I am your handmaid and your relative by marriage."

"Oh," said Boaz, "That's all right then. You are a good girl and I will be a good kinsman to you. Now lie down again till morning."

She did and then crept away early, before, we are assured, there could be any hanky-panky.

All the same, Boaz made it clear that he would rather people didn't know that a woman had slept at his feet all night. There might have been talk.

The next part of the story is all about selling and buying land and the upshot was that Boaz not only bought up a lot of land but also bought Ruth (we are not told from whom or for how much) and married her.

They all lived happily ever after.

And Keats wrote these lines in 'Ode to a Nightingale'

> Perhaps the self-same song that found a path
> Through the sad heart of Ruth, when, sick for home,
> She stood in tears amid the alien corn.
> The same that oft-times hath
> Charm'd magic casements, opening on the foam
> Of perilous seas, in faery lands forlorn.

(I'm not competing with Keats, but I'm not sure if he got it right about Ruth being sick for home.)

DANIEL

This story brings three well-known sayings - 'feet of clay' and 'law of the Medes and Persians.' 'the writing on the wall'.

In the reign of Nebuchadnezzar, the Hebrew Daniel was much favoured as an administrator.

The king was also very impressed with three Jewish characters called Shadrach, Meshach and Abednego.

(Rather mysteriously they started the story with different names and changed to these for no apparent reason.)

"They are ten times better than all the other astrologers and magicians," he announced.

Nebuchadnezzar had a dream which disturbed him so much that he summoned all the wise men and gave them an ultimatum.

"Interpret my dream correctly and I will reward you with wealth beyond the dreams of avarice, but if you fail I shall have you chopped into small pieces."

This was alarming enough, but the next condition was even more chilling.

"If you are any sort of magicians or soothsayers or astrologers you will be able to tell me what the dream was and then interpret it."

This unreasonable request completely floored the wise men which so annoyed the king that he ordered them all including Daniel, to be cut into pieces.

Daniel went to the king and asked for a little more time, during which he would find out the dream and interpret it. This the king granted.

Daniel went home and consulted Shadrach, Meshach and Abednego and together they prayed to God to let them know what the dream was. This God did, so at least they had something to work on.

They asked Arioch who had been given the job of cutting the wise men into small pieces to hold his hand, as they were about to interpret the dream.

Arioch rushed Daniel to the king where he offered to say what the dream was and then interpret it.

The dream is rather complicated, but it seems to have been of a monster image made of gold, silver, brass and iron. The feet were a mixture of iron and clay and were broken into pieces.

This, said Daniel, foretold a series of kingdoms, some more and some less powerful, but ultimately the final kingdom would be the Kingdom of God.

"Your god is obviously top god," said the king, and made Daniel governor of Babylon with Shadrach, Meshach and Abednego as his assistants.

Nebuchadnezzar's next act was to have an enormous golden statue made. It was sixty cubits high and six cubits wide and was erected in the province of Babylon. A cubit was about 18 inches, so it was an enormous statue - about 90 feet high and nine feet wide.

The king's herald blew his trumpet and announced:

"Everyone, when they hear the music of the cornet, flute harp, sackbut, psaltery and all kinds of music, must fall down on their faces and worship this splendid golden image which the king has erected at his own expense. Anyone failing to comply will be cast into a burning fiery furnace"

Obviously, the Jews weren't going to do that. They failed to fall down on their faces when they heard the music of the cornet, flute, harp etc. and were reported to the king by some sneaky Chaldeans.

"Sire, there are certain Jews in positions of authority who did not fall down on their faces when they heard the sound of the cornet, harp, flute etc. Their names are Shadrach, Meshach and Abednego."

Nebuchadnezzar summoned the three Jews.

"Is it true?" he asked," that when you heard the sound of the cornet, harp, flute etc., you did not fall down and worship the golden image which I made at my own expense? If you did not I'm afraid you're for the fiery furnace."

"So be it," replied the three men. "With any luck our god will deliver us from the fiery furnace."

This made the king extremely angry and he ordered for them to be flung into the fiery furnace. In fact, it was to be heated to seven times its usual fiery heat.

The Jews were cast into the furnace which was so hot that the men doing the casting all died.

Undeterred by the extreme temperature they proceeded to utter prayers and praise God for the next three pages and were not even singed.

Nebuchadnezzar was very impressed and issued a decree that anyone speaking against Shadrach, Meshach or Abednego would be cut into small pieces.

Shadrach, Meshach and Abednego,
Now there's a trio of
Unforgettable names.
Lovely rhythmic names which make
A trochaic quatrain
If I'm not mistaken.
Dum de-dum, de-dum, de-dum-de.
But finding a rhyme for the last name.
Is challenging.
'To bed we go', of course.
But hard to make use of
And not suitable for a serious piece of verse.
What about adapting Sidney Carton's
Last words from The Tale of Two Cities?
Shadrach, Meshach and Abednego

> Looked in the furnace and said, "We go
> To a hotter place than we have ever been.
> A far far hotter place than we have ever known."
>
> *On second thoughts, perhaps not.*

Soon after this Nebuchadnezzar had another dream, this time it was of an immense tree which reached up to heaven. It bore delicious nourishing fruit which fed people and animals for miles around.

Then came a voice from heaven, saying, "Cut down the tree, scatter its fruit, let nothing remain but a stump."

"Oh, dear!" said Daniel. "I'm afraid it means that if you do not mend your ways, after the success and prosperity of your early reign, you will be displaced, become homeless and forced to eat grass like an ox."

"I don't think so," said Nebuchadnezzar. "I am king of great Babylon and invincible."

"No, Nebuchadnezzar – you are about to be deposed. You will live in the fields, eat grass like an ox – and this will go on for seven years until you realise that God rules over the kingdoms of men and can dispose of them as he wishes."

And that's what happened. Nebuchadnezzar was made homeless and forced to live on a diet of grass. Not only that, his hair turned into feathers and his fingernails into claws. He repented of his pride then. Who wouldn't?

The next king we meet is Belshazzar, Nebuchadnezzar's son. He organised a tremendous feast for a thousand of the great and the good.

He ordered wine to be served in the vessels looted from the temple in Jerusalem and compounded this sacrilege by praising idols made of gold and silver.

While they were carousing in this manner, a disembodied hand appeared and wrote on the wall in fiery letters: MENE MENE TEKEL UPHARSIN.

This so upset the king that he started to tremble and his knees knocked together. "Send for the astrologers and wise men," he cried. "Whoever can explain this writing shall be richly rewarded with fine clothes and become the third most important person in the kingdom."

They sent for Daniel who came and gave Belshazzar a piece of his mind.

"Your father was a great king, he had the power of life and death over his people, but in the end God humbled him and he was reduced to eating grass like an ox. I'm sorry to say that you are treading the same path. You have taken vessels from God's temple in Jerusalem, you've worshipped idols of gold and silver. Now I'll tell you what the fiery words mean.

MENE MENE   God hath numbered thy kingdom and finished it. TEKEL -thou art weighed in the balance and found wanting- UPHARSIN – thy kingdom is divided and given to the Medes and Persians.
It is clearly a very succinct language.

That very night Belshazzar was killed and Darius, a Mede (Persian), took the kingdom.

Darius admired Daniel and made him the head of a triumvirate of presidents who in their turn controlled one hundred and twenty province governors. These governors resented a Jew in this exalted position and plotted his downfall.

Together they went to Darius and suggested he should issue a decree that anyone, during the next thirty days, who bowed down and worshipped anyone or anything save Darius himself should be cast into a den of lions.

"Sign the decree, your Majesty so that it is unalterable according to the law of the Medes and Persians."

Darius obediently signed and the plotters at once went to Daniel's house where they found him praying.

They hurried back to the king and told him that he had got to cast Daniel into the lions' den because he, the king, had signed an unbreakable decree.

Very reluctantly Darius agreed; he felt he had no option; the law of the Medes and Persians is sacrosanct.

Daniel was duly thrown into the lions' den and a great stone was rolled over the entrance and sealed with Darius's own seal. Darius spent a very unhappy night and early the next morning ran down to the den to see what remained of Daniel. To his delight he found Daniel alive and well.

"Oh, Daniel," he said, "your God is quite something."

He then ordered all the plotters to be thrown into the lions' den together with their wives and children.

Altogether a very satisfactory ending.

ROUGH JUSTICE

Nothing is more pleasing
Than seeing the wicked
Get their comeuppance.
I suppose some sensitive souls
Might raise questions
About the wives and children
Who joined their husbands and fathers
In providing the lions with supper
And might have felt a bit
Hard done by.

No, no, the sins of the fathers
Must be visited on their children.
They must be discouraged
From having criminal dads.

SUSANNA & THE ELDERS

This is the story in which Daniel is the hero for saving an innocent woman from injustice. This is where he gets his reputation for wisdom quoted by Shylock in The Merchant of Venice "A Daniel come to judgment"

Scene 1 (Joachim's walled garden)

Susanna and her maids are walking in the garden. The two Elders who are looking out through a window watch her with greedy eyes.

ELDER ONE
Good-looking woman, eh?

ELDER TWO
Certainly is. Good job we're a couple of old has-beens. *(laughs unconvincingly)*

ELDER ONE
No, not for us I'm afraid. Not the sort of thing we should be thinking about. Ha ha!

ELDER TWO
Well, I must be toddling off – I'll probably see you here tomorrow?

ELDER ONE
I dare say – there are always legal problems with old Joachim.

The Elders go off, but sneak back separately and peer over the garden wall at Susanna, still strolling about.

SUSANNA *(to her maids)*
Look, girls, it's terribly hot, I really do need to freshen up. Would you go and

fetch me water and soap and a towel and then make yourselves scarce.

The Elders overhear this and waggle their eyebrows suggestively.

The maids return with the water and then leave when Susanna takes off her top and starts to wash.

The Elders come bursting in through the garden gate as fast as their aged legs will carry them.

ELDER ONE
Hello, dear. What a lovely creature you are to be sure. We've got a little proposition for you – Be nice to us both if you know what we mean.

ELDER TWO
Yes, dear. Be really nice to us and we won't mention that young man you were canoodling with after you sent your maids away.

SUSANNA *(indignant)*
What are you talking about? I haven't been canoodling with anyone!

ELDER ONE
You know that and we know that, but the judges only know what we shall tell them. Our word against yours.

ELDER TWO
Guess who they'll believe. A couple of respected Elders or a sexy young woman? Come on! Be a sport!

SUSANNA
Oh God! I'm done for whichever way I turn. Is there no help for me? *(she looks up at the sky and walks frantically up and down)* NO! Not in a million years! I'd rather stick pins into my eyes than be touched by you horrible wrinkled old sacks of dung.

ELDER ONE
I think you'll find what's coming to you is rather more serious than pins, my dear. Come, brother, let's to the judges.

Scene 2 (Court room.)

USHER
All stand!   *(Susanna is brought in with her hands bound)*

JUDGE
You are accused of adultery by these two eminently respectable and credible witnesses. How do you plead?

SUSANNA
Not guilty, your Honour.

JUDGE
Call the witnesses.

ELDERS *(speaking in turn)*
We happened to be looking over Joachim's garden wall and we saw this woman engaged in sexual congress with a young man under a tree. We rushed in to apprehend him but he was too nimble for us and escaped over

the wall. However, we arrested this adulterous woman you see before you. Shame on you woman!

JUDGE
Open and shut case. The woman is clearly guilty of adultery. Punishment is death, to be carried out immediately!

Susanna is seized and is being dragged away when the young Daniel jumps to his feet.

DANIEL
Stop! Stop this instant! Are you such fools? This is a mockery of a court of law. Who has examined the witnesses? Have you, m'lud?

JUDGE
Er- no.

DANIEL
Allow me, please. Have the two witnesses separated, I shall examine them apart. *(Elder 2 is taken out of the court room.)*

DANIEL *(to Elder one)*
You say you saw the accused engaged in sexual congress with a young man under a tree?

ELDER ONE
Yes, and a disgusting sight it was.

DANIEL
And under which tree was this act taking place?

ELDER ONE
Er – under the mastic tree.

DANIEL
Thank you. Take this witness outside and bring in the other Elder. *(Elder 2 is brought in)* You say you saw the accused engaged in sexual intercourse with a young man.

ELDER TWO
Yes, I did. I certainly did.

DANIEL
Did you enquire of the accused what the young man's name was?

ELDER TWO
Of course. But she refused to tell us.

DANIEL
I think you said this act was taking place under a tree?

ELDER TWO
Yes, and a disgusting sight it was.

DANIEL
Can you remember which tree it was?

ELDER TWO
Er – yes, it was the holm-oak.

DANIEL *(to judge.)*
These men are clearly lying m'lud.

JUDGE
You're absolutely right. *(To warders)* Take these men away and chop off their heads and be quick about it!

CURTAIN

(Loud and sustained applause)
More comeuppance.   Splendid!

Yes, serve them right, dirty old men!
Those Peeping Toms were at it again.
Remember them before you go
Window shopping in Soho.

JOB

The Book of Job contains an immensely long philosophical poem with some splendid lines like;

'Man is born to trouble as the sparks fly upwards.'

Once upon a time in the land of Uz there lived a man called Job (pronounced Jobe) who was perfect in every way. He had seven sons and three daughters. He had huge flocks of sheep, great herds of camels and five hundred yoke of oxen, not to mention five hundred she-asses and innumerable servants and retainers.

In short, he was an extremely successful wealthy man, who was also both pious and virtuous, never failing in his religious duties.

However, there was a summit meeting in Heaven which was attended by Satan.

"What have you been up to, Satan?" asked God.

"Going to and fro on the earth and walking up and down on it."

"Did you by any chance come across my servant Job?" enquired God, "He's unequalled, there's no one like him on earth for sheer perfection and loyalty to Me."

"H'mm," said Satan, "That's all very well, but you've protected him, blessed him with good things and made him rich. If you were to take that away you'd soon see how much he loves you."

"You're on!" said God, "Do what you like with his belongings, but don't hurt him."

Off went Satan and quite soon unpleasant things began to happen.

A marauding party of Sabeans killed Job's ploughmen and made off with the oxen.

A fire came down from heaven and consumed all Job's sheep and shepherds.

A party of Chaldeans killed the camel drivers and stole the camels.

A tornado struck Job's house as his children were eating dinner together. The house collapsed and they were all killed.

Job wept but he was stubborn.

"The Lord gave and the Lord taketh away, blessed be the name of the Lord."

Soon there was another heavenly summit. This time God asked Satan what he had been doing and got the same answer.

"What about my servant Job? You didn't get very far with him, did you?"

"That was just possessions," replied Satan, "If he was touched in person it would be a very different story, he'd renounce you quick enough."

"You're welcome to try," said God. "Do what you like but spare his life."

Job was then afflicted from head to toe with the most horrible boils which he tried to scrape off with a bit of broken crockery.

"For heaven's sake," cried his wife, "why are you still determined? Renounce God and die!"

"Don't be foolish, woman. If we accept good from God we should also accept evil."

The next fifty pages are spoken by Job and his three friends in the form of a very long series of poems, full of superb language but extremely wordy. They try to comfort him by pointing out his weaknesses and they certainly don't satisfy God, who gives them a severe ticking-off. You have done a lot of talking, but you haven't spoken of what is right, and Job has. Go away and sacrifice seven bullocks and seven rams and Job will pray for you.

So *'Job's comforter' has entered the language to describe sympathy which makes things worse.*

Job, like Abraham, had passed the test and was rewarded with double the number of animals and servants that he had before.

The ten dead children and the shepherds seem to have been forgotten. Well, they were dead anyway and Job was in clover.

JOB

Job was a biblical billionaire
With enormous flocks and herds
He was never short of a suitable prayer
Couched in suitable words.

God was exceedingly pleased with Job
He was God's sort of man.
But Satan, that well-known deophobe
Came up with a devious plan.

"He's only religious because he is rich.
And lives without transgressions.
He'd chuck his religion into the ditch
Without all his possessions.

"All right," said God, "put him to test
Deprive him of his riches.
I bet that he will come out best
Though stripped down to his britches."

Satan took God at his word
Blew everything to hell,
Camels, sheep and cattle-herd
Daughters and sons as well.

Patient Job remained steadfast
Though gripped in Satan's coils.
So, Satan's final blow was cast,
Afflicting him with boils!

Job's comforters then came to call
Or so the story runs.
"Why don't you just end it all?"
But Job stuck to his guns.

Thus God beat Satan for a change
And Job was doubly blessed.
His lands were doubled in their range
His flocks and herds were best.

MORAL
Now, though we 're often driven
To question God's fair play,
We must accept: 'What God hath given
God may take away.

JONAH & THE WHALE

Jonah, well-known as a prophet and preacher, was instructed by God to go to Nineveh, which had the reputation of being a particularly wicked city and get them to change their ways. For some reason Jonah was reluctant to do this - perhaps he was nervous about preaching in such an evil place. Instead, he decided to take a boat to Tarshish.

God was not having such disobedience and sent such a mighty storm that the boat was close to foundering. The sailors were sure that someone on board was causing the storm and drew lots to find out who it was. The lot fell upon Jonah.

"Who are you? Where do you come from? What's your job?" enquired the crew.

"It's all my fault," said Jonah. "Cast me into the sea!"

The men were loath to do this, they struggled to get to land but it was in vain. So, over the side went Jonah.

But God was keeping an eye on him and sent a mighty fish which swallowed him up. For three days he remained in the belly of the whale. From there he sent up a heartfelt prayer professing his loyalty to God and the whale vomited him up onto dry land.

For the second time God told him to go to Nineveh and sort that wicked city out. Jonah didn't need telling again and set off for Nineveh.

Now he was Jonah the prophet.

"In forty days," he cried, "you are all doomed. Nineveh will be destroyed!"

Amazingly, they believed him and at once started to repent. The king issued a proclamation saying that everyone was to fast: men, women, children and animals. "Sackcloth and ashes for all!" he ordered, "it's just possible that God will change his mind and not destroy us."

God approved of this and decided not to strike them down with fire and brimstone.

You'd think Jonah would be delighted at the success of his mission but far from it. He went into a sulk and, presumably because of the slur to his professional reputation as a prophet, complained to God.

"You might just as well take my life," he whined, and went and sat down outside the city wall.

Far from taking his life God caused a gourd to grow over his head to shelter him. This was very welcome when it was too sunny or raining.

God then caused the gourd to wither and die.

"Are you sorry the gourd has died?" he asked.

"Yes, I am. Very!"

Well, if you are sorry for the death of a gourd, how much sorrier you should be for the death of a whole city of eighty thousand souls and a lot of animals."

We are not told what Jonah said, if anything. He might have said that he was not particularly sorry for the death of the gourd, but he was sorry to lose his shelter.

PROFESSIONAL PRIDE

The professional pride of a prophet
Is something we should not despise.
A prophet whose prophesies go wrong
Will not be regarded as wise.
Jonah had called down brimstone and fire,
Delivery in forty days.
Then God quite suddenly changed his mind.
No lightning or firework displays.

Pretty galling for Jonah's professional pride
No wonder his mood was not good.
He'd expected to wipe out a decent-sized city.
He felt foolish and misunderstood.

―――――

But Jonah! Nineveh mended her ways.
Shouldn't that count as a plus?
It was your preaching that turned them around
So kindly stop making a fuss.